LITTLEHAMPTON
A Pictorial History

The Front, Littlehampton, *c.*1870.

LITTLEHAMPTON
A Pictorial History

D. Robert Elleray, A.L.A., F.L.S.

Phillimore

1991

Published by
PHILLIMORE & CO. LTD.
Shopwyke Hall, Chichester, Sussex

Tel no. 01243 - 787636

ISBN 0 85033 769 0

Printed and bound in Great Britain by
BIDDLES LTD.
Guildford, Surrey

For Audrey Robinson and Mary Engel

List of Illustrations

Frontispiece: The Front, Littlehampton, c.1870.

Preface and Acknowledgements

My earliest recollections of Littlehampton are of childhood – being taken into a shop, I think in Pier Road, by an indulgent uncle and presented with a model yacht, which I immediately launched in the Oyster Pond! This was in the 1930s and much has changed in the town since then although, happily, the sense of a community preserving much of its traditional identity still survives. Coming to describe Littlehampton after examining other Sussex seaside places, the town presents yet a further variation on the resort theme – each one, Eastbourne, Worthing and the rest bringing its local character to form a picture of that special type of town which developed in the late 18th century – the sea-bathing place. So Littlehampton makes its own special contribution to an intriguing story and I hope the following pages will portray this and encourage readers to explore the town's history and become active in conserving its character.

For help received in my research my sincere thanks go to Carolyn Brown, B.A., and Oliver Gilks, B.A., (former curators, Littlehampton Museum) for their courteous and resourceful assistance, and also to Miss Iris Jones and Captain D.A. Ward (former Harbourmaster). In addition to photographs and material from my collection I am indebted to the following for permission to copy illustrations: Beckett Newspapers (Copyright Plate 152); Father John Bloomfield; Mr. Tyndall Jones; Mr. J. E. Gammon; Littlehampton Museum; Mrs. A. E. Moore; the National Monument Record; Mary Taylor; and Mr. J. Wetter. I am grateful to Miss Esme Evans for typing the manuscript, and to David Nicholls (Worthing) for undertaking part of the photographic work.

D. Robert Elleray
Littlehampton, November 1990

Littlehampton has trebled its population since 1801, and now contains upwards of 1600 inhabitants. This ... is owing to its having became a resort for sea-bathing, for which it possesses sufficient facilities, and is rather a favourite place with those who prefer quiet and retirement.

J. D. Parry, *The Coast of Sussex*, 1833

On the occasion of my visit I fell in with a party of Old Littlehamptonians who had come back to hold a 'Back to Littlehampton Day', and as we went along they remarked on the progress that had been made. Even the ruined windmill, they said, was twice the ruin it was in their day.

Max Murray, *c.*1925

Introduction

The Harbour

Littlehampton port may be classified together with Newhaven and Shoreham as an estuary harbour, all three having been stimulated into various degrees of expansion when the railway development of the mid-19th century brought the opportunity of cross-Channel trade. In Littlehampton's case, however, the stabilisation of the mouth of the Arun had proved a recurrent problem from medieval times until the Victorian period, necessitating frequent attention and expenditure to ensure normal operation.

The history of Littlehampton as a port functioning chiefly as an access to Arundel goes back to the distant past. William Prichard notes that Littlehampton was 'an acknowledged port of ancient date',[1] and by 800 the river was navigable to Arundel, a military station. In 1066 the import of Caen stone for use at Arundel Castle is recorded, and in 1071 the port was recognised by the Crown. Hakluyt refers to the construction of war ships at Littlehampton by Henry VIII, no doubt utilising Sussex oak. The emergence of Arundel port as pre-eminent seems to have been due to improvements carried out in the 1570s by the Earl of Arundel, Henry Fitzalan, who embanked the lower section of the Arun and diverted its course, bringing it close to the castle, and so providing a convenient location for wharfage. These improvements had included a new 'cut' to the harbour entrance at Littlehampton, but by 1640 the constant drifting of shingle was again blocking the river mouth and pushing it eastwards.[2] Later in the century conditions improved but by 1730 the harbour had only five feet of water, and in 1732 a petition was made to Parliament via Sir John Shelley requesting remedial measures. Action was soon taken and the following year the Arundel Port Act was passed, which appointed commissioners and authorised an engineer, John Reynolds, to carry out work. This included a new cut 500 yards west of the existing mouth, which was described as 'venting itself in several places'. Two piers were also built to impede drifting shingle, and operations were completed in 1735. Difficulties persisted, however, and periodic work continued: in 1793 a second Act extended the piers and provided a tow path to Arundel, and in 1825 a third Act authorised the use of £20,000, to deepen the harbour. Some idea of the appearance of the harbour entrance at this period is given in Cox's picture of about 1830 (*see* plate 4). It appears that some form of harbour defence existed in Tudor times, probably on the east bank, and in 1759-60 a battery was established a little west of the present Coastguard Station. This was removed in the 1830s. In 1854 a fort was built on the west bank, but it was hardly used, and was dismantled *c.*1900.

By 1800 the bias of the Port Commissioners in favour of Arundel was evident: of the 74 commissioners, 48 came from Arundel and only five from Littlehampton! Their efforts to maintain Littlehampton harbour were purely to ensure easy passage up-river to Arundel. In spite of attempts to retain traffic at Arundel, however, only one quarter of the annual tonnage arriving at Littlehampton was reaching Arundel by 1824, due mainly to the opening of the Wey and Arun Canal in 1816. This event was decisive in the ultimate decline of Arundel Port and the success of Littlehampton. Even so facilities at Littlehampton were modest: in 1801 only the Town Quay existed at the end of Surrey Street, subsequently the timber wharf of John Eede Butt (now Travis Perkins), but by 1804 shipbuilding was well established and two firms, Corney and Carver, and Isemonger, were employing 36 men. Some related industrial building was also appearing and in addition a number of houses in Surrey Street, a few of these still surviving today, mainly erected by seafarers and merchants. By 1825 further quays were in use and in the same year a platform ferry,[3] designed by John Skirrow, stimulated activity in the port area, but although some expansion was achieved, the general development of both harbour and town was depressed and, it would appear, waiting for a rail link to be constructed. In 1846 distant railway facilities were provided at Lyminster, but 17 years were to pass before a branch reached the town and harbour in 1863.

With the railway came a new chapter in the harbour's history and its rise to importance with the decision of the L.B.S.C.R. to introduce a cross-Channel boat service from Littlehampton. The line opened in August 1863, with a station strategically sited near High Street and in proximity to the harbour. This allowed trains to reach the riverside where the railway company purchased land for train and boat operations. The effect on the town was immediate and the consequent prosperity marks the emergence of modern Littlehampton and the amalgamation of three elements – village, port and resort – into one community. The L.B.S.C.R. had already opened services to the continent from Shoreham (1843) and Newhaven (1847), and a service in conjunction with Henry P. Maples began from Littlehampton in November 1863, constituting, in the words of the *West Sussex Gazette*, 'an important addition to our district, by the establishment of a continental steam packet service by the first cargo boat, the *Vibourg* from Jersey and St. Malo ... and the *Rouen*'.[4] During 1864 another company, the Littlehampton, Harve and Honfleur Steam Ship Co. operated a service using chartered ships.[5] No doubt as a result of these new services the commissioners allowed the Customs House to be transferred to Littlehampton, reflecting the changed relationship between the two ports. Yet the years of successful steam packet operations from Littlehampton were numbered and the increasing competition from other south coast ports led to profitability virtually ceasing after 1877, when net profits were only £398, plummeting to a loss of £3,290 in 1879. The situation boded ill for the survival of the railway steamers, and even more ominous was the Company's decision in 1878 to commit major investment for development at Newhaven, thus making it economic to concentrate services there in 1882 and abandon Littlehampton. So ended the promise of the harbour as a cross-Channel port, and despite a varied coastal trade, especially in coal and Baltic timber imports, a gradual decline began in the port's fortunes, which continued (except during the First World War) until 1927, when under the terms of the Littlehampton Harbour and Arun Drainage Outfall Act, the Commissioners were disbanded and West Sussex County Council was empowered to fund the operation of a Harbour Board.

The decline of Littlehampton port since the cross-Channel years should not detract from the sustained activity of local shipbuilding and seafaring families and their achievements. Local shipbuilders were active during the last quarter of the 18th century: Thomas Isemonger is mentioned in the 1770s as probably being involved in constructing sloops for the Royal Navy, and in 1793 he was appointed first harbour pilot. Other shipbuilders of the 19th century were Corney and Carver, Stephen Olliver and Henry Harvey. Henry Salter's plan of the harbour in 1841 indicates the position of the old ship yards and Littlehampton Museum displays numerous paintings of the harbour and the ships built there.[6] The outstanding name among Littlehampton's seafarers is Robinson, members of the family dominating the town's maritime affairs during most of the 19th century, and it was appropriate that the former home of Captain Arthur Robinson housed the town's museum during the years 1969-91. The family originated in Pagham and it was from there that the young Joseph Robinson, aged 15, walked to Littlehampton in 1835 seeking an apprenticeship with Thomas Isemonger. He was unsuccessful, but only a short time elapsed before he went to sea, and later Joseph founded the shipping company G. and J. Robinson, which flourished until the 1920s.

Early in the First World War the Railway Company briefly ran a steamer service between Littlehampton and Dieppe, but this ceased when the harbour increasingly became used for exporting war materials to France. The use of the port during the Second World War was much less, consisting chiefly of maintaining light air-sea rescue and patrol boats, and later the preparation of landing craft for D-Day. Some exercises for this historic event took place on the west beach. Both landing craft and 'Fairmile' motor gunboats had been constructed during the war by William Osborne Ltd., a firm established at Littlehampton in 1919.[7] After the war their yards became known for the production of motor yachts and especially, from 1949, for lifeboats, launching the first self-righting example, the *J. G. Graves of Sheffield* in 1958. A total of 52 lifeboats were built or fitted out by 1981. During recent years the growing popularity of the harbour as a yachting centre with a flourishing club has been reinforced by the formation of a Marina which has led to a considerable increase in summer activity. Less fortunate has been the extension of industrial development in the area defined by the loop of the new bridge opened in 1973. Recent years have seen harbour import trade maintained at a level of about 350,000 tons per annum and its position can be described as reasonably successful although the present plans for Surrey Street urban development may not be in the best interests of port operations and could destroy its traditional atmosphere.

The Resort and Town

Describing Littlehampton in 1965, Ian Nairn said that the town was 'pleasant but exasperatingly disjointed ... a rather bewildering mixture of Old Hastings and Bournemouth' – words correctly suggesting the differing elements which have combined to form the modern town: village, harbour and resort. The fact that a harbour of medieval date has formed an integral part of Littlehampton's development gives the town some similarity with Hastings and Brighton and sets it apart from Sussex resorts of more straightforward origin such as Bognor, Eastbourne or Worthing; it is also significant that of the three Sussex ports, Newhaven, Shoreham and Littlehampton, it is only Littlehampton which has successfully incorporated a resort in its development.

Littlehampton provides an example of a river-mouth settlement and the east-west axis of High Street probably derives from the ancient track linking the church with a ferry, and forming part of the Brighton-Bognor road. This, together with a south-west branch to the river-mouth (Surrey Street), formed a basic street pattern, only to be slightly modified by later urban development towards the coast, *c*.1800. Settlements of earlier date existed in the immediate area and evidence such as the Romano-British finds on the Courtwick Farm Estate in 1951 and Beaumont Estate in 1965 confirm this, such farmsteads gradually amalgamating to form the village.[8] By 800 the river was navigable to Arundel and during the Saxon period the Manor of Hantone, assessed at one hide, was held by the sister of Edward the Confessor, Countess Goda, later passing to Earl Roger de Montgomerie. In 1562 the manor was purchased by John Palmer of Angmering, and in 1712 by the Duke of Norfolk, the whole forming the Norfolk estate of modern times. The medieval village of Littlehampton was a community with interests divided between agriculture and fishing, with increasing activity on the river to Arundel gradually extending its influence on the area. By the 14th century a church, manor and a small group of dwellings existed around a triangular green or market place furnished with a pump and pond. This layout is still recognisable today between Manor Parade (formerly Island Terrace, demolished 1964), the Manor House and the line of old cottages opposite. Originally the track running from this point to the river was 'West Street', later becoming High Street. But the growth of Littlehampton was slow, reflecting the comparative isolation caused by the river and the extensive marshy area – the Black Ditch or Dike – to the north, these conditions often making communications difficult. By the end of the 17th century the village was described as having only 14 dwellings, the extension of building westwards along High Street towards the river being a slow process, but eventually accelerating in response to the growing importance of the harbour. Here growing maritime prosperity led in the late 18th century to modest industrial and other development around the Town Quay, River Road and Surrey Street. A further factor in village growth was the increasing use of the east-west Brighton-Bognor road, which focused interest on the ferry, especially when it became a turnpike road in 1825. Despite these developments and the trend towards resort activity in the later 18th century, the local government of the village remained a leet jurisdiction – administered by the Vestry – no commissioners being appointed before the creation of a Board of Health in 1853.

The Resort

The date of Littlehampton's emergence as a seaside resort appears to have been comparatively early, seabathing having begun in the 1750s. In 1764 the *Sussex Weekly Advertiser* was announcing holiday accommodation and good seabathing, and by 1778 there were four bathing machines in use and some 30 bathers. By this time activity was centred on the Beach Hotel Coffee House, built in 1775, where basic assembly room facilities were provided by a William Jefferies. The Coffee House was described as 'built on a kind of sandbank approaching so near the tide that many have been apprehensive lest the sea should make an unmannerly attack and enter the room ...', an interesting comment on the state of the Green at that time and suggesting a reason for the later seafront being set so far back from the sea. Further comments were made by a lawyer, Peregrine Phillips, when he arrived at the inn in August 1778.[9] Anticipating primitive accommodation, he was 'agreeably surprised to be introduced into a lofty parlour ... in a hansome, large, well-built house ... above 100 yards from the edge of the ocean' where he partook of 'a cheerful repast completed by a bottle of excellent port'. Phillips' remarks on Littlehampton are vivid, Mr. Jefferies being 'a good, honest, well-tempered obliging fellow', and he notes that 'the Dukes, the Corneys, the Scarvels, the Hentys and the Isemongers have by intermarriage peopled the whole village'.

In 1788, the town's first entrepreneur, Peter Le Cocq, a successful Parliament Street coffee-house owner, arrived to promote the resort and, using his London connection, began to expand the comforts at the *Beach Hotel*. On 27 July 1789 the *Sussex Weekly Advertiser* announced that 'Mr Peter Le Coq most respectfully informs the nobility and gentry that there will be a public breakfast at his new room on the beach, Littlehampton on July 30';[10] and again, 'on August 10 ... a public ball'. To this is added: 'Peter Le Coq thanks the nobility and gentry for their support at the breakfast ... there will be one every Thursday during the season'. Le Cocq's new facilities included a long room complete with gothic windows and furnished for both assemblies and Roman Catholic worship – apparently in deference to the wishes of the Lord of the Manor – the Duke of Norfolk! In this way Le Cocq had successfully launched Littlehampton as a Regency resort and, following his death in 1797, his wife Rebecca continued in charge until 1813. By this time a road (now Beach and Granville roads) existed from the east end of High Street down to the hotel. In all probability this would have become the main street leading to the resort, but in 1790 circumstances arose which deflected the development further eastwards.

In 1790, Frederick Augustus, fifth Earl of Berkeley, decided to build a secluded residence at the east end of the Green, later purchased by the Earl of Surrey and known as Surrey House. This important building, according to John Cole Tompkins 'the commencement of Littlehampton',[11] decided the future location of 'Beach Town' and established the line of South Terrace (thus ensuring the survival of the Green) which thereafter extended westwards reaching the river just over a century later, in 1897. By about 1814 a Regency-style terrace stretched from Norfolk Place to just beyond Norfolk Road, where a short line of smaller houses ran up the east side with a narrow street behind the terrace. This constituted the resort of 'Beach Town', lying a considerable distance south-east of the village, the name continuing in use until c.1900. The chronology of the terrace may be gleaned to some extent from William Clift's drawing of 1822, now in the Museum. Here the similarity to development at Eastbourne is striking, where 'Seahouses' became established south-east of the old village of Bourne. Fortunately Beach Town survives as a most interesting example of a miniature resort, and still retains some of its original atmosphere. In his diary Tompkins records visiting Littlehampton with the Duke of Norfolk to discuss the 'building of a row of new houses west of Lord Berkeley's', and it appears that the Duke made two grants of manorial land for housing c.1797 and 1804. This raises the question of the influence of land ownership in resort development, and again Eastbourne and Littlehampton may be compared to provide a striking contrast. In the first instance the Duke of Norfolk played a more passive rôle, and although supportive to growth in Littlehampton, only occasionally becoming involved in town affairs, with gifts of building sites.

Meanwhile the resort was increasing in reputation: a bath house had been erected, coaches ran to London, Brighton and Worthing, and a theatre opened in 1807. A large new church, St Mary the Virgin, opened in 1826, and in 1832 the *Brighton Gazette* referred to band concerts, boat races and racing on the sands. In 1829 the Earl of Surrey gave £100 towards 'the cost of a new carriage road from the Beach Hotel to the Church – an improvement much desired by locals ...'. So Littlehampton steadily turned into a 'delightful and retired watering place', the least pretentious of all south coast resorts – no vulgarity, no apeing of Brighton. In Richard Dally's words it was 'well adapted for family parties, whose enjoyments begin and end in their own circle'.[12] During these early years of development, 1801-41, the town's population had grown from 581 to 2,270.

The next twenty years witnessed relative stagnation in company with a number of other resorts. The census figures for Littlehampton in 1861 showed an increase of only 80 persons over the 1841 count, despite the opening of a station on the Brighton to Chichester line at Lyminster in 1846 with a horsebus service to the town.[13] It was not until 1863, following the decision of the railway to build a branch to the town and open a cross-Channel boat service, that the modern phase of Littlehampton's development as a resort began. The new conditions created employment, and housing began around the railway station and at Wick. In 1866, the town's leading architect, Robert Busby (1813-

91)[14] began to extend South Terrace and behind it Western Road, the group including nine houses with distinctive semi-circular bays – reminiscent of the Busby and Wilds style of Regency Brighton. By the 1870s the terrace had reached St Augustine Road but, apart from the isolated Selbourne Place (1869), a considerable 'green belt' still separated Beach Town from the village. In 1880 the Duke of Norfolk laid the foundation stone of the Water Works and in 1881-2 a new water and drainage scheme was completed, an obvious prelude to future urbanisation, the local press commenting that 'we hope to see early signs of building operations at Littlehampton'. This hope was fulfilled and during the next 25 years the remaining rural area yielded to spaciously laid out housing centred on a wide avenue, Fitzalan Road, but fortunately leaving Caffyns Field, north of the Roman Catholic church, as a kind of 'village green' surrounded by genteel late Victorian and Edwardian villas. In 1887 the long-requested loop line at Ford was opened, ending the tiresome shunting of trains then necessary, and facilitating tourist access. As elsewhere such changes and the arrival of the excursion trains were greeted with mixed feelings by residents and often strongly opposed. In June 1887 the *South Coast Visitors Journal* bluntly stated that there was '... little doubt that the Sunday Excursions ... are sources of evil to the town rather than good – a bad feature is their repulsiveness to the class of people who choose quiet watering places to visit ...'. Others complained that the 'beautiful Common was gradually disappearing under the hands of the builders and the townspeople all eager that Littlehampton should become a fashionable seaside place'. Despite such complaints these years are now considered a halcyon period and become the object of nostalgia – as in the words of Osbert Lancaster 'the *unbutlined* Littlehampton of those days represented the English seaside at its best'.[15] In 1893 when the population was nearing 5,000, the town's status was enhanced by creating it an Urban District Council, and in the next thirty years, except for the First World War, a steady progress continued until 1930, when the population topped ten thousand. The following year a significant change occurred when the Duke of Norfolk, reacting to financial pressures, sold much of his Littlehampton estate to a London developer, although the Council had already negotiated the purchase of the Green, foreshore and Arun Mill the year before.

Yet another significant change was to hit the town in 1931: Butlinisation! In that year the highly sensitive area on the east bank, comprising the Arun Mill and old Battery site, was acquired by Butlin's for an amusement park, and its transformation soon began with the demolition of the Mill in 1932. This act of vandalism, later regretted by Billy Butlin, drew indignant comment from Frazer Hearne: 'Littlehampton Windmill, for so long a characteristic feature of the place has been razed to the ground in order to make room for a Whoopee City!'.[16] But the change was welcomed by others, perhaps less discriminating, as a boost to Littlehampton's prosperity. The *Sussex Daily News* backed the project with enthusiasm, stating that 1933 would 'always be remembered as the year the town came into its own ... in this respect Littlehampton owes a great deal to a fairy godfather, proprietor of the Amusement Park which has caused thousands of visitors to pour in by road and rail, packing the beach and foreshore to a density hitherto unknown or even undreamed of ... Littlehampton has truly lived up to its motto of 'Progress' in 1933'. To crown this wave of prosperity the Southern Railway completed its electrification to Littlehampton in 1938. This somewhat hectic period was cut short by the Second World War when the town found itself in the front line, with air raids, threat of invasion, and the port in use for air-sea rescue and the assembly of landing craft for the landings in Normandy. Following this hiatus Littlehampton was left with the familiar problems of rehabilitation, and decisions concerning its future rôle and identity as a viable community.

Littlehampton since the War

In September 1944 the beaches were reopened and a return to normality began as a trickle of visitors appeared in the town. In 1948 attention turned to the future of the Littlehampton Estate, residual parts of the Norfolk Estate, which was being sold with Council support to George H. Upjohn, with outline proposals for a 10-year development to benefit Littlehampton and raise the population to 30,000. At the time when 'new towns' were being built, such ideas gained support and the *Sussex Daily News* commented that such a scheme, incorporating 'the surrounding villages of Clymping, Ford, Rustington, Angmering, East Preston and Lyminster, would offer great scope for the planning of a fine modern seaside resort'.[17] Fortunately the coast was spared this urbanisation and eventually progress towards a 'structure plan' for the area lessened, to some extent, the threat of unacceptable development. Controversy arose however in 1962-3, when an appeal was allowed to erect housing on the east side of the town, a decision leading to amalgamation with Rustington and destroying any chance of preserving a green belt north of Mewsbrook. The quality of the resulting estates was mediocre and aptly described by Michael O'Halloran as 'standard, unimaginative design coupled with dreary planning'.[18]

Perhaps moved by the appearance in 1962 of a scheme from the Rodwell Town Development Group, which would have destroyed Littlehampton as we know it, a town centre map was produced by the County Council proposing a phased introduction of relief roads north and south of High Street. Nine years were to elapse, however, before a Local Plan (1973) appeared suggesting the road changes should be implemented 'in such a way as to create a more attractive townscape ... fitted into existing development with due regard to scale and setting', but then remarking that 'there are very few buildings of architectural interest in the town centre' – a doubtful judgement in the context of plans seeking to enhance the traditionally-built environment of the town. So far only the north relief road (Franciscan Way) has materialised, leaving an all too familiar scar across the town.

The 1980s opened with the demolition of the Methodist church in New Road and later Auklands Holy Family Convent School in Norfolk Road, and a large open space was sacrificed to housing. But the main focus of attention during the decade has been on projects which, if fulfilled, will alter fundamentally the character of Littlehampton. One of these, the bypass, has already caused major environmental upheavals on the northern fringe of the town with associated out-of-scale industrial building in Wick, and especially the gigantic Watersmead complex at Toddington – an outstanding blot on the landscape. On the western side of the town a new development, 'Fishermans Quay', of over eight acres and centred on the ancient town quay area, is threatening the *Britannia Inn* and the long neglected Floyds corner terrace. A successful appeal against demolishing these buildings in late 1990, however, may well modify the future of this area.

In conclusion it appears that Littlehampton, like many other towns, approaches the end of the century with a growing threat to its character and traditional atmosphere as a resort. At the moment the greatest natural advantage the town still enjoys is the unspoilt countryside on the west bank of the Arun – the only surviving example of natural coastline in West Sussex. Yet the growing pressure to initiate some form of development in the marina area is very real and the only way of countering the threat is an unequivocal policy to resist any further development on the west bank. Unhappily ambivalence prevails on this vital point in the Draft Plan of 1989, and so the future of Littlehampton's traditional setting, so correctly perceived and encouraged by Peter Le Cocq 200 years ago, now hangs in the balance. It is hoped that the quiet, unobtrusive but highly successful tradition of the town's progress will be fully appreciated and respected in decisions concerning future change.

1. Richard, William B., *A Treatise on Harbours ... on the South-eastern coast of England*, Vol. 1, Fisher, 1844, p.46.
2. The transformation of the Arun mouth has broad similarities with Shoreham and is the subject of a number of theories e.g. by Allcroft, and others.
3. A ferry was provided in Henry IV's time by the Dudley family. (*S.N.Q.* 16 p.239.)
4. 19 Nov. 1863.
5. Farrant, *Mid-Victorian Littlehampton*, p. 5. *See also* Hart, H. W., 'Littlehampton to Honfleur', *Journal of the Railway & Canal Historical Society*, Vol. 8, No. 1, Jan. 1962.
6. Preserved in Littlehampton Museum.
7. Morris, J., *The Story of Littlehampton Lifeboat Station*.
8. Report by Cutler, *Sussex Archaeological Collections*, Vol. 92 (1954), p.38.
9. Phillips, Peregrine, *A Sentimental Diary in a Month's Tour from London to Littlehampton ...*, 2 vols., J. Ryall, 1778.
10. By a local builder, J. Tupper.
11. *Sussex Archaeological Collections*, Vol. 71 (1930), p.48.
12. Dally, p.234.
13. The Company's undertaking to build a branch to Littlehampton was not carried out.
14. *Littlehampton News*, 21 Oct. 1891.
15. *All Done from Memory*, 2nd ed., 1963, p.46.
16. *Sussex Archaeological Collections*, Vol. 74 (1933), p.25.
17. 12 May 1948.
18. *Financial Times*, 28 Sep. 1968.

Bibliography

Aldsworth, Fred G., 'A Description of the Mid 19th-Century Forts at Littlehampton and Shoreham ...', *Sussex Archaeological Collections (S.A.C.)*, Vol. 119, 1981, p. 181-94

Allcroft, A. Hadrian, *Waters of Arun*, 1930

Allnutt, A. G., 'Littlehampton Swing Bridge', *Sussex Industrial History (S.I.H.)*, No. 12, 1982

Apostolic Schools, *Short History of the School of Littlehampton Sussex (Formerly Schools of Amiens and Boulogne)*, c.1890

Arun District Council Planning Department, *Arun District Local Plan: the draft plan October 1989*, 1989

Arun District Council Planning Department, *Climping Gap Consultative Document – Summer 1989*, 1989

Arun District Council Planning Department, *Littlehampton Harbour: a development strategy for the future*, 1985

Batho, I., 'A Holiday in Littlehampton 1788', *Sussex History*, Vol. 2, No. 4, 1982, p. 4-10

Blick, F. N., 'Romano-British finds on the Beaumont Estate, Littlehampton', *Sussex Notes and Queries (S.N.Q.)*, Vol. 17, 1971, p. 112-5

Budgen, W., 'Littlehampton Hot Baths', *S.N.Q.*, Vol. 1, 1927, p. 227-8

Burrows, G. S., *Littlehampton Town Centre: a local plan*, 1973

Challen, W. H., *Parish registers*, *see* Robinson, Eva, and Heward, J. S.

Cotham, William, *A Survey Book of the Manor of Littlehampton with Toddington, 1633, see* Steer, Francis W.

Daggett, Ilene and Wilfred, *Toddington (West Sussex) Its Past and its People*, 1987

Dally, Richard, *Bognor, Arundel and Littlehampton Guide ...*, 1828

Davies, C. P., 'The *Clympings* built at Littlehampton', *West Sussex Gazette*, Nov. 26, 1970

Farrant, John H., 'A Bridge for Littlehampton 1821-2', *S.I.H.*, No. 5, 1972-3

Farrant, John H., *The Harbours of Sussex 1700-1914*, 1976

Farrant, John H., *Mid-Victorian Littlehampton: the railway and the Cross-Channel Streamers* (Littlehampton Papers No. 4), 1977

Goodliffe, W., *Littlehampton, Arundel and Amberley ...*, 1916

Goodwin, John, 'Arundel Haven: a history of Littlehampton fortifications', *In the Military Defence of West Sussex*, 1985, p. 21-42

Hulme, E. Wyndham, 'Portbooks and customs accounts of Arundel and Littlehampton in the Tudor period', *S.N.Q.*, Vol. 9, 1943, p. 106-8

Johnson, G. D., 'Arun mouth ford', *S.N.Q.*, Vol. 17, 1970, p. 198-9

Johnson, G. D., 'The Mouth of the Arun', *S.N.Q.*, Vol. 15, 1960, p. 149-54

Johnston, Philip M., 'Notes on an early map of Atherington Manor (and description of the) ancient chapel (Bailiff's Court)', *S.A.C.*, Vol. 44, 1901, p. 147-66

Jones, Iris, *Wartime Littlehampton, 1939-40*, 1989

Jones, Iris, and Stanford, Daphne, *Littlehampton in old photographs*, 1990

Lock, Henry, *Memoirs (c.1882), see* Thompson, Herbert, *The Early 19th Century* (Part One)

Maitland, J. Pelham, 'The Medieval Church of St. Mary the Virgin', *S.A.C.*, Vol. 5, 1935, p. 199-202

Mitchell & Son, *Guide to Littlehampton ...*, 1847

Morris, Jeffrey, *The Story of the Littlehampton Lifeboat Station ... with a brief history of William Osborne Ltd ...*, 1981

Murphy, C. C. R., *Log of a Lymphad*, 1939

Newman, Ronald F., *Monumental Inscriptions in the Parish Church of St. Mary the Virgin Littlehampton* (Littlehampton Papers No. 3), 1970

Ockendens, *One Hundred & Fiftieth Anniversary Souvenir Catalogue*, 1952

Peckham, W. D., 'Littlehampton Vicarage', *S.N.Q.*, Vol. 12, 1948, p. 49-51

Phillips, Peregrine, *A Sentimental Diary in a Month's Tour from London to Littlehampton ...*, 2 vols., 1778

Prichard, William B., 'Arundel Port and Littlehampton', *A Treatise on Harbours ... on the South-eastern coast of England*, Vol. 1., 1844

Robinson, A. W., 'A Family Firm of Sussex Shipowners. The Story of the Robinsons of Littlehampton', *Sussex County Magazine*, Vol. 12, 1938, p. 30-2 and 91-5

Robinson, Eva and Heward, J. S., *Reminiscences of Littlehampton with map 1852 and transcripts of the Parish Registers A.D. 1611-1753 by W. H. Challen*, 1933

Robinson, Joseph Richard, *Reminiscences*, 1963, transcribed by Audrey Robinson, manuscript Littlehampton Museum

Sams, Valerie Stevenson, 'Littlehampton in Retrospect', *Sussex County Magazine (S.C.M.)*, Vol. 22, 1948, p. 77-8

Shorter, George, 'Littlehampton Harbour', *S.C.M.*, Vol. 27, 1953, p. 416-22

Smart, Nevil, *The Visitors Guide to Littlehampton*, 1879

Steer, Francis W. (ed.), *The Manor of Littlehampton with Toddington, 1633* (Parts 1 and 2) (Littlehampton Papers Nos. 1 and 2), 1961

Thompson, Herbert J. F., 'Beside the Sea at Littlehampton', *West Sussex History*, No. 22, 1982, p. 14-19

Thompson, Herbert J. F., *The Early 19th Century* (Part One), 1983

Thompson, Herbert J. F., *Littlehampton long ago*, 1974

Thompson, Herbert J. F., *Littlehampton Through the Wars* (The Littlehampton Story No. 1), 1978

Thompson, Herbert J. F., *The Swing Bridge Story* (The Littlehampton Story No. 2), 1979

Thompson, Herbert J. F., *The Picturemakers* (The Littlehampton Story No. 3), 1981

Thompson, Herbert J. F., *Then and Now* (The Littlehampton Story No. 4), 1982

Thompson, Herbert J. F., *What's in a name?* (The Littlehampton Story No. 6), 1988

Van Heyningen Brothers Ltd. Toddington Nurseries, *Van Heyningen Brothers: 25 Years of Success, 1964-89*, 1989

Vine, P. A. L., 'Arun at Littlehampton', *London's Lost Route to the Sea*, 1986

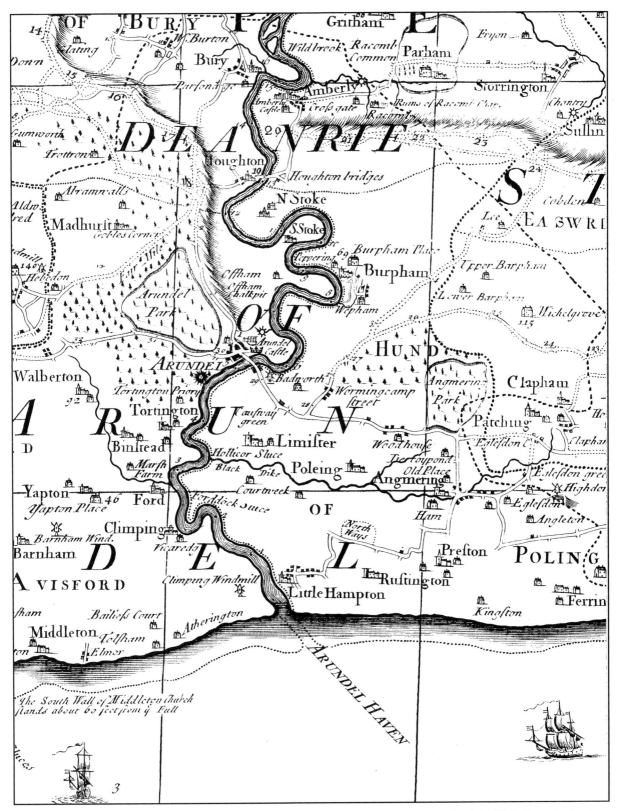

1. Richard Budgen's map of 1724 showing the Littlehampton district. The east-west axis of the High Street is clearly indicated and also the swampy 'Black Dike' area, which often hampered effective communications to the north.

2. Possibly the earliest view of Littlehampton – the 'Beach Coffee House' and Long Room, published in *The Topographer* in 1791. The mill, built *c*.1740 or before, was removed in about 1825.

3. Surrey House, which stood until 1948 just east of Norfolk Place, was the most important building in the resort development of Littlehampton. It was erected by the Fifth Earl of Berkeley in 1790.

4. The harbour entrance *c.*1816 – a drawing by David Cox.

LITTLE HAMPTON

IS a sea-port, market town and parish, in the hundred of Poling and rape of Arundel, four miles south from that town, situated on the east bank of the river Arun, on the coast of the English channel. This place, which, about twenty-five years since, was but a small fishing village, is now a sea-port of some importance, and, as a bathing place, annually advancing towards celebrity. The fineness of the sands, the limpidness of its waters, and the salubrity of the air, have for some time caused it to be resorted to as a watering place; and many fine buildings have been erected along the shore, in situations commanding most extensive prospects, including

Brighton, on the coast, the Isle of Wight, more distant; and, on the land side, much beautiful and varied scenery. There are several inns, distinguished for the excellence of their accommodations; the shops are fitted up with great taste; the reading-rooms are well supplied; and the baths embrace hot, cold, shower, and shampooing. The principal trade, besides that derived from visiters, is in coal and timber. The commercial prosperity of Little Hampton has of late been considerably increased by the operations of two new ship-building establishments that are carried on with great spirit; one by Mr. Stephen Olliver, the other by Mr. Thomas Isemonger. Belonging to the works of the first named gentleman is a new slip and powerful steam engine, employed in towing in vessels of any burthen, that may require immediate attention; these works are approached by a ferry: the other yard, an extensive one, is situated in the town. It is in contemplation to establish a fishery here for mackarel and herrings; and the harbour being one of the best along this coast, it may be fairly presumed that Little Hampton will shortly become a place of considerable commerce, as well as being held in high estimation as a place of summer resort.

The church, dedicated to St. Mary, is in the early style of English architecture; the benefice is a vicarage, in the patronage of the see of Chichester. The charities comprise a school for the education of twenty boys, founded by a Mr. John Coney, and a benefit society, established in 1815, for affording relief to the aged, indigent and infirm. A corn market is held on Thursday, which is well attended. Population, in 1831, 1,625.

POST OFFICE, Thomas Phillips Cox, *Post Master.*—Letters from LONDON and all parts arrive (by way of Arundel) every morning at 9, and afternoon at half-past one, and are despatched every afternoon at five.

NOBILITY, GENTRY AND CLERGY.
Appleby Mr. Edward John
Batty Mr. William
Bethell Mr. Richard
Blake Mrs. Elizabeth
Bonnett Thomas, esq.
Coombes Mrs. —
Delafield Rev. John
Dyer Mrs. Ann   [notary]
French Mr. Robert (attorney and
Gibbons Mr. Richard Howard
Gilkes Rev. William
Greatly Major Thomas
Keale Captain —, R. N.
Lillywhite Mr. Peter
Marshall Mr. Charles
Olliver John, esq.
Scarvell Mrs. Jeremiah [house
Surrey Right Hon. the Earl of, Surrey
Swan Mr. Hugh   [R. N.
Thorndike Lieut. Charles Augustus,
Wilder Rev. John
Woolley Mr. Thomas

ACADEMIES.
Cox Thomas Philip. (boarding and
  day and general agent)
Grix John (boarding & day) [ing]
Harwood&Overington(ladies'board-
Isemonger Misses (boarding)
Simpson George (day)

BAKERS.
Carter Robt. (& miller & corn factor)
Dudding William (and confectioner)
Gibbs John (& confectioner), Beach
Marshall William (and biscuit)
Simpson Robert
Willishear Charles

BOOT AND SHOE MAKERS.
Coake Charles | Sanders Robert
Graysmark Thos. | Shelley Zachariah
Howard Cornels. | Slaughter George
Marshall George | Wheeler Henry

BRICKLAYERS.
Tupper James (and plasterer)
Tupper Thomas (and plasterer)

BUILDERS.
Butt John, jun. (and brick maker)
Henry John, Peckham

BUTCHERS.
Blake Charles
Corney Stephen
Duke Richard
Bushby Robert

CARPENTERS.
Corney Edward (and undertaker)

CHYMISTS AND DRUGGISTS.
Smart Nevil (and stationer and sub-
  distributer of stamps)
Spencer William Henry

COAL MERCHANTS.
Coake Charles (dealer)
Corney George (and rope maker)

GARDENERS.
Simpson James (and seedsman)
Wood Alexander (and seedsman)

GROCERS AND DEALERS IN SUNDRIES.
Gales Francis
Leggett William Henry (and draper)
Sparks & Son (and drapers)

HOTELS & PUBLIC HOUSES.
Beach Hotel, Leah Tupper
Dolphin Hotel and Commercial Inn,
  Henry Richard Richards
George (posting and commercial),
  William Robinson
King's Arms, James Cooper
New Inn, Henry Henly, on the Beach
Norfolk Hotel (posting and commer-
  cial), Henry Binsted Locke
Ship & Anchor, George Green
White Hart, James Blackaller

IRONMONGERS.
Butt John (and china, &c. dealer)
Ockenden William

MERCHANTS.
Isemonger Richard & Son (and de-
  puty vice-admirals and agents for
  droits of admiralty)

MILLINERS.
Burry Jane
King Fanny (and dress maker)

PAINTERS' & GLAZIERS.
Denyer William
Freeman John
Keywood James
Swan John

SADDLERS.
Cooper George
Heward John

SHIP & BOAT BUILDERS.
Isemonger Anthony (boat)
Isemonger Thomas (ship)
Olliver Stephen (ship); New slip

SHIP OWNERS.
Isemonger Rd. & Son (& ship agents)
Love Edward

SMITHS.
Green Benjamin
Ockenden William

SPIRIT MERCHANTS.
Applegate Robert (brandy)
Duke James

STRAW HAT MAKERS.
Cunningham Mary & Sarah
Dorwood Eliza
Whitmarsh Phœbe

SURGEONS.
Candy John Henry
Evans Owen
Wallington Thomas, Beach

TAILORS AND DRAPERS.
Breese Timothy (and hatter)
Dyer William (and hatter)
Pepper Edward

Miscellaneous.
Carver Robert, harbour master
Chatfield Absalom, wheelwright
Constable George Sefton, brewer&maltster
Corney John, fire office agent
Downer George, dairyman
Ede John, hair dresser and perfumer
Edis Mary & Susan, library, Beach
Gales Elizabeth, ship chandler
Hammond Henry, brazier and tinman
Jubb Spencer, corn merchant&barge owner
Keywood James, currier
Lawson Richard, wharfinger
Lear Henry, accountant
Lemon George, lime burner
Miller Rupert, sail maker
Mitchell Ruth, stay maker
Osborn William Arthur, cabinet maker
  and upholsterer
Paine John, shipsmith   [Inn
Robinson Edward,coachproprietor,George
Slaughter Samuel, town crier
Stummer George, cooper
Tidey John Fryer, surveyor, auctioneer
  and billiard rooms, Beach
Wood Peter, watch and clock maker

COACHES.
To LONDON, the *Comet*, from the Norfolk Hotel, every morning at ten—and
  the *Royal Sussex*, from the George,
  every morning (Sun. ex.) at half-past ten.
To BRIGHTON, the *Royal Sussex*, every
  forenoon at eleven; goes thro' Worthing.
To CHICHESTER, the *Royal Sussex*,
  every evening at seven.

CARRIERS.
To LONDON, James Keywood, from his
  yard, every Monday and Thursday—and
  Brook's Van, from the Norfolk Hotel,
  every Tuesday and Thursday.
To BRIGHTON,—Collins' Cart, from
  the Dolphin, every Monday & Thursday
  —a Van, from the George, every Tues.
  & Thurs.—and Wm. Laiter, Friday.
To CHICHESTER, George Green, from
  the George, every Tuesday & Thursday.
To PORTSMOUTH & SOUTHAMP-
  TON, G. & W. Pescott, from the George,
  every Monday and Wednesday.

CONVEYANCE BY WATER.
To LONDON & CHICHESTER, Spen
cer Jupps' Barges, every Saturday, to th
Three Cranes wharf, Upper Thames st

5. The description of Littlehampton published in Pigot's *Sussex Directory* in 1838. Note the daily coach services to London, Brighton, Worthing and Chichester from the *Norfolk* and *George* inns.

6. Doctor John H. Candy, the town's leading physician during the latter part of the 19th century. He lived for a time at the Manor House, and served as Chairman of the Local Board, 1855-8, and again in 1865-78.

7. Autographed photograph of Henry Fitzalan-Howard, 15th Duke of Norfolk (1847-1917). Educated at the Birmingham Oratory, he succeeded in 1860 and served as Postmaster General, 1895-1900. The Duke played a part in Littlehampton affairs, and among several benefactions were the sites for the Hospital, Library and sports ground.

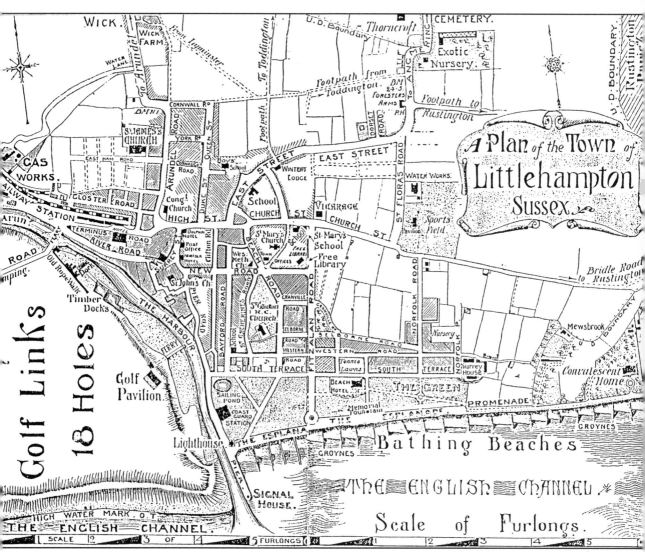

8. Map of Littlehampton in about 1905, showing the west end of South Terrace completed, East Ham Road laid out, and the area between Fitzalan and Norfolk roads as yet undeveloped.

9. A Newman print *c*.1870 of the beach and harbour. In the centre distance is the West Beach fort, and just visible, to the right of the lighthouse, Clymping windmill.

10. Littlehampton Harbour in the age of sail, from a folding guide of *c*.1870.

11. Littlehampton Harbour painted by S. Poulson *c.*1852 is perhaps the best 19th-century topographical painting of the port. Both atmosphere and detail are excellent – even to showing the rather dangerous warp in the chimney of Harvey's shipyard.

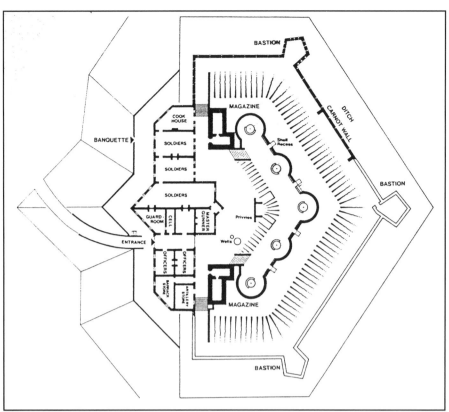

12. The west bank fort was built in 1854 at a cost of £7,615 and was intended to be manned by one gunner, two officers and 42 men from other ranks. Armament consisted of three 68-pound and two 32-pound guns. The fort was dismantled *c*.1900.

13. Steam and sail in the harbour in about 1900. On the right is the Norwegian *Augusta*, registered at Haugesund, and in the distance the *Arun View Inn* close to where the swing bridge was later erected.

LITTLEHAMPTON HARBOUR.

14. The Arun Commissioners *en bateau* in 1887, William Sewell, Harbour Master, by the flag. The Commissioners, appointed in 1732, strongly promoted the interests of Arundel over Littlehampton until about 1840 and were later superseded by the Harbour Board.

15. A view of Littlehampton harbour after the turn of the century.

The Pier, Littlehampton

16. Edwardian scene at the harbour entrance showing the jetty, proudly referred to as the 'Pier'! The decorative lighthouse was later replaced by the severely functional concrete tower in use today.

17. First World War scene at Littlehampton harbour, showing the unloading of captured German artillery pieces from France in 1918.

18. An L.B.S.C.R. poster timetable for the London-Honfleur steam packet service via Littlehampton in 1869. It operated from 1863 until 1882 and brought considerable prosperity to the town.

London Brighton & South Coast Railway Co.

NOVEMBER, 1869. NOVEMBER, 1869.

LONDON & HONFLEUR
Via LITTLEHAMPTON,
BEING THE
SHORTEST ROUTE TO CAEN, TOURS, & THE WEST & SOUTH-WEST OF FRANCE.

The Screw Steamers "RENNES," "CAROLINE," & "IDA" are appointed to sail with Passengers and Merchandise as under (weather and unavoidable circumstances permitting), in connection with the London Brighton and South Coast Railway and the Western Railway of France.

CATTLE CAN NOW BE IMPORTED AT LITTLEHAMPTON FOR THE INTERIOR.

THERE ARE NO PIER DUES OR CLEARING CHARGES AT LITTLEHAMPTON.

TERMINUS BRIGHTON.

19. The *Steam Packet Inn* near the Swing Bridge – its name is now the only visible reference to the former steamboat service to the continent during the years 1863-82.

20. In 1824 an Act was passed to provide a ferry over the Arun. It opened in June 1825. The platform barge was built by Thomas T. Isemonger, and the chain winding mechanism by Bramah (London) from designs by John Skirrow. Piles for the 1908 bridge appear on the left.

21. The Duke of Norfolk in festive mood at the opening of the old swing bridge in May 1908.

22. Notice of the official opening of Littlehampton Bridge in May 1908, and the public luncheon, during which music was provided by 'The Blue Hungarian Band'. On the back is 'The Song of the Bridge', specially composed by the Vicar of Clymping.

New Bridge. Littlehampton

23.   The provision of a swing bridge for Littlehampton in 1908 was an important event and indicated the town's growing prosperity. But there was opposition to the plan resulting in a referendum in which the 'Bridgers' polled 675 against the 'Anti-Bridgers'' 213!

24.   The first consignment of timber to cross the newly-opened swing bridge in May 1908. A nicely posed photograph with everyone watching the camera, including the horses and the dog!

25. The elderly John Harvey, well-known local shipbuilder, passing the time of day with a sentry on the swing bridge during the First World War.

26. William Arthur Butt in about 1875. His father John Eede began as a builder and later became a major importer of timber at Littlehampton and Shoreham. The last survivor of the family, Charles, died in 1962.

27. The main wharf at Littlehampton in about 1946. One of the chief imports, coal, ceased in 1951, and today aggregates form the basic trade.

28. The new footbridge over the Arun opened in 1982 at a cost of £500,000. It has a 120-ton retracting centrepiece which is used some 600 times a year. The design was by Redpath Dorman Long.

29. The harbour in 1989, showing the extensive accommodation for yachts along Rope Walk. The distant gas-holder replaced a much smaller one after the last war.

30. Historic Ferry House, River Road, was deliberately set on fire in 1987 and now awaits demolition. Possibly a remodelling of a 17th-century building, it was once occupied by a branch of the Robinson family.

31. Captain Louis Robinson who died in 1962, aged 86. He
commanded the Robinson's last sailing ship, the *Ebenezer*, for
13 years. In 1911 Captain Robinson was wrecked at South
Shields in the *Constance Ellen*.

32. The *Ebenezer* was built by May of Shoreham in 1860.
After being sold in 1915, the *Ebenezer* was sunk by a
submarine in 1917.

33. Surviving early 19th-century warehouses in River Road, an area now threatened by the 'Fishermens' Quay' development.

34. The *Britannia Inn* near the Fisherman's Hard. Although much altered it dates from *c.*1800, and is threatened by the new quayside development.

35.   Ennerdale House, River Road, was built by the local seafarer Captain Arthur Robinson in 1912, and later (1966-91) provided an appropriate setting for the town's museum. Owing to financial stringencies the museum recently moved to the Manor House.

36.   The Summer House in the former museum garden, together with the Long Gallery, were erected and carved by Captain Robinson from old ships' timbers after his retirement in the 1920s.

37.   The energetic tug *Jumna* in action *c.*1905. Behind can be seen the pier light, which together with the matching lighthouse, were locally called the 'pepper and salt'. The tug was built by Hepple at North Shields in 1884 and worked at Littlehampton from 1887 to *c.*1923. Later she was sold and used on the Tigris and Euphrates.

38.   The old *Glen Rosa* paddle steamer entering the harbour in about 1912. She was built by Caird of Greenock in 1877 and later purchased by Campbell's, being broken up after war service in 1914-18.

39. The *Brighton Belle* entering the harbour alongside the 'Pier'. The 'pepperpot' lighthouse added much to the visual quality of the port entrance but was unfortunately removed during the Second World War.

40. The arrival of a new lifeboat, the *Brothers Freeman* in 1904, was the occasion for great festivities in the town. She is shown here being paraded through Surrey Street and High Street preceded by the town band.

41. Launching the Littlehampton lifeboat, *Brothers Freeman*.

42. Old cottages and lobster pots in Pier Road before the First World War. The cottages – 'Mussel Row' – were rebuilt in 1929.

43.   Mussel Row, Pier Road, Littlehampton, *c.*1927.

44. The crew of the lifeboat *Brothers Freeman*, a photograph taken in about 1905.

45. The *Lapstone*, said to have been used by smugglers in 1830, served as a dwelling ('Noah's Ark') next to the *Arun View Inn* until removal in 1908 after the construction of the swing bridge.

DEMOLISHING BY
BEN CRUBB.
GOVERNMENT STORE DEALER.
445 & 447 Commercial Rd.
Phone 2731.   Portsmouth.

WHEN IT'S WET · IT'S FINE AT BUT

46. The fine Arun tower mill on the east bank was the harbour's most distinctive landmark for just over a century. Built in 1831 by Henry Martin, a Bognor miller, it was run by John Woodhams for many years. The mill ceased working in 1913, and was demolished by Butlin's in 1931.

47. The sad end of the Arun Mill in 1932, when it was demolished to enlarge the Butlin's site which for some time was known as the 'Windmill Amusement Park'.

48. Second World War landing craft lying on the west bank prior to the D-Day landings in 1944.

49. Osborne's offices in Rope Walk. This well-known firm was established in 1919, and has since become famous for the construction of cabin cruisers, yachts and especially lifeboats.

50. The Coastguard Station lookout tower east of the river-mouth was erected in 1931. On the left is the extension added in 1986 at a cost of £70,000.

51. Children at the Oyster Pond in about 1910. The pond was formed around 1798 to store the local catch, and as a storm water reservoir. In 1895 it was converted into an ornamental boating lake. The picturesque background of the Arun Mill and coastguard buildings is now replaced by the bleak north wall of Smart's.

52. A water-colour by Edwin Harris showing the sea front in about 1860. Of particular interest is the bath house (left, south-west of the *Beach Hotel*), once an important part of the sea bathing facilities provided by the early resort.

53. A Rock lithograph of the old *Beach Hotel* in about 1875. In 1887 the present hotel was built to the east and the two stood side by side for a short time until demolition of the original inn.

54. A photograph *c*.1880 of the old *Beach Hotel* and South Terrace. A fragment of this old building still survives in the present hotel's garden. ~ this hotel demol. 1994

55. The *Beach Hotel* in its heyday *c*.1910. It remained the town's premier hotel for many years but is now closed, and the fate of this fine 'Queen Anne'-style building is uncertain.

56.   The highrise interloper, Kingmere, a development by Cubury (London) completed in 1970. Its height does great harm to the surrounding area, especially to Selbourne Place and the *Beach Hotel*.

57.   Beach Town's original seafront – a delightful line of Regency houses built on an intimate scale, and successfully combining both brick and stucco.

58. A view of Surrey House *c.*1870 when run as a school by John Grix, and later George Neame. After 1885 the house became a hotel and was occupied later by Lady St Maur. Military use during the Second World War did great damage but the house deserved restoration because of its historical importance.

59. Norfolk Place, part of the Regency development west of Surrey House. The central building with pediment is modern and replaced the original stable block *c.*1972.

60. Thomas Henty of Church Farm, West Tarring, pioneer sheep farmer. In 1829 he sailed from Littlehampton to Australia in the 340-ton *Caroline*, complete with family, farm equipment and staff. The livestock included Merino sheep which he reared in Australia.

61. The historic *New Inn*, Norfolk Road, built about 1803 and seen here *c.*1914, has important connections with the Henty family and Australia. In June 1829 Thomas Henty held a farewell party at the inn before his departure to New South Wales.

62. Originally called 'The Hillyers', the Mary MacArthur House is the grandest Regency house in South Terrace and was once run as a boys' academy by the Rev. W. Philpott. After the war until 1964 it became the Princess Louise Children's Hospital, and then for a time the Mary MacArthur Holiday Home for Working Women.

63. The fine gothic-style fountain erected on the Green by the town to commemorate the accession of Edward VII. Unfortunately it seems to have been removed during the Second World War.

64.   Edwardian beach scene at Littlehampton. In the top left-hand corner is the old *Bellevue*, later *Southlands Hotel* (1866), demolished in 1948, now Southlands Court.

65.   Holiday crowds on the Parade in about 1905. In the background is the 'pepperpot' lighthouse and the west bank fort, dating from 1854 and now demolished.

66.   The popular Littlehampton Miniature Railway in the 1960s, when it was worked by a number of fine steam locomotives. The railway was opened by Mr. Leslie Turner in 1951 and run by him until 1969.

67. The sea frozen at Littlehampton beach during the great frost in late January 1907.

68. The first parish church, St Mary's, as illustrated in the *Gentleman's Magazine*. The fine 14th-century east window on the left is now in the tower of the present church.

69. Littlehampton's second parish church, designed by George Draper (of Chichester) in 1826, cost £3,000, including a donation of £100 from the Duke of Norfolk. Its generous proportions reflect the growth of the town and the anticipation of further resort development.

70.   Interior of St Mary's, showing the 1826 nave and Victorian chancel before remodelling in 1934, which introduced stone arcading. The prominent monument (top right but now relocated on the south wall) commemorates John Grix (died 1861), master of Surrey House School.

71.   The third parish church was consecrated in 1934 – a remodelling in red brick by Randoll Blacking in a style described by Pevsner as 'eerie disembodied Gothic'. The large interior with galleries retains monuments from the former churches.

72. Rural Church Street in about 1890, near the present junction of Goda Road, which was laid out in 1907. Goda, sister of King Ethelred II, held land in the Littlehampton area before the Conquest.

73. The Friends Meeting House, Church Street, one of the most attractive buildings in Littlehampton, with delightful gothic detailing. It was built as an infant school in 1835 by Mrs. Sarah M. Welch, and Henry Lock taught there for several years. On the left is Regency Cottage.

74.   A print dating from the 1860s showing the new Congregational chapel and Manse designed by J. G. Stapleton. The Manse (centre, now rebuilt) was destroyed by bombing in August 1942, when the Minister and his wife, Mr. and Mrs. Hailstone, were killed.

75.   Farm buildings at the bottom of Arundel Road in about 1830, the site later chosen by the Congregationalists to erect their chapel in 1861. The founders were Samuel Evershed and Thomas Duke.

76. Photograph looking east along High Street showing decorations marking Queen Victoria's Golden Jubilee in 1887. On the right is the *Dolphin Hotel* (rebuilt in 1938) and in the distance Constable's brewery chimney.

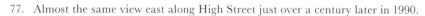

77. Almost the same view east along High Street just over a century later in 1990.

78. High Street looking west in about 1926. On the right can be seen the gateway to The Lodge, occupied by the Constable family until its demolition to make way for the Odeon cinema, in 1931.

79. Smart's Corner and High Street in about 1890. The shop, originally leased from Thomas Constable in 1836, became an institution under the versatile direction of Nevil Smart who operated as chemist, wine merchant, newsagent, vet and tobacconist rolled into one!

80. Smart's Corner and High Street in 1990, showing the shop little altered since the late 18th century, and the pedestrianisation of High Street completed in 1981.

81. Everything for the thirsty Victorian holidaymaker at Littlehampton! An advertisement from Smart's *Guide* published in 1879. Nevil Smart opened his well-known shop in 1836, and it continues today.

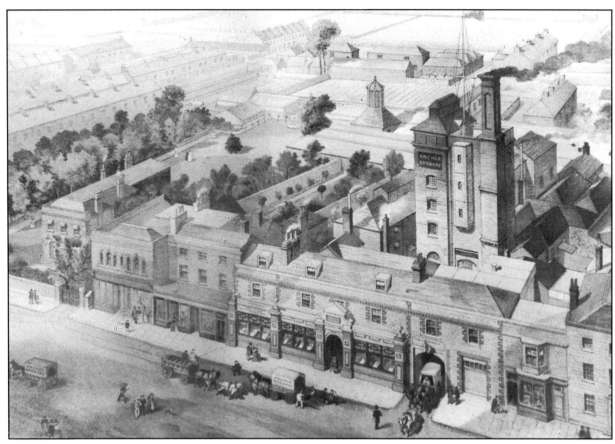

82.   Constable's Brewery. A brewery had existed in High Street since *c.*1845, and was purchased by John Constable in around 1853. After 1917 only mineral water was produced and in 1921 the firm amalgamated with Henty and Constable of Chichester.

83.   The attractive knapped and cobbled flint façade of Peter Dominic's High Street shop is all that remains of the old Constable's Brewery. The large tower and chimney at the rear were demolished in 1972, just over a century after erection.

84. *(Above left)* Archibald J. Constable, owner of the High Street brewery, was Chairman of the Urban District Council 1904-11. He was the nephew of the founder, Thomas Constable, who died in 1885.

85. *(Above right)* George Groom, a successful grocer, came to Littlehampton in 1892, taking over Ellison's in High Street. He opened three more shops in the town but later sadly took to drink with fatal consequences.

86. *(Right)* By far the most stylish building in High Street is the National Westminster Bank, built in red brick with elaborate stone dressings and turret.

87. The workforce of Constable's Anchor Brewery, High Street, in about 1900.

88. Until the construction of Franciscan Way, Duke Street had a good array of 19th-century flint buildings. The *Globe Inn*, shown here, is one of the few survivors after clearance for car parking.

89. Surrey Street in the 1870s, showing the *Norfolk Hotel* which was built in 1825. Beyond is the notorious 'Floyds Corner', the town's only Georgian terrace, built *c*.1784, with fine pedimented doorcases, and now derelict after years of neglect.

90. Advertisement for the *Norfolk Hotel*, Surrey Street dating from about 1890.

Hoad-Quarters of Littlehampton Sailing Club.

The Norfolk Hotel

SURREY STREET,

LITTLEHAMPTON.

The most central and near to Station.

Family and Commercial.

An Ordinary every Day at 1 p.m.

One of the Finest Billiard Saloons in the Town.

Agent for Salt's Burton and Constable's celebrated Littlehampton Ales and Stout.

Extensive Livery and Bait Stables.

T. A. HILL,
Proprietor.

91. The old *Norfolk Hotel*, Surrey Street, *c.*1860. Once the town's premier hotel it continued until the Second World War and its demolition robbed Littlehampton of an historic building.

92.   The Surrey Street fair, seen here *c.*1920, provided one of the most colourful events in the town's calendar, until growing traffic problems caused its suspension after May 1933.

93. Stage-coach travellers at the *White Hart*, Surrey Street, *c.*1890. The inn is first recorded in 1761 as the *Swan*, changing its name to the *Dolphin* in 1772. In 1784, the present *Dolphin* opened nearby, necessitating a final change to *White Hart*. Alterations to the front date from *c.*1925.

94. Two 18th-century buildings in Surrey Street – the Cairo Club and (left) Old Quay House, displaying a fine doorcase. This house is presumably the end building of the once elegant red brick terrace beginning at 'Floyds Corner'.

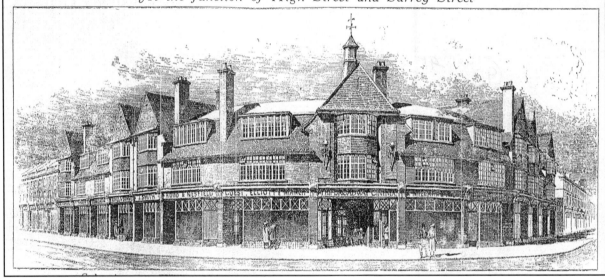

Littlehampton's Important Public Improvement Scheme
At the Junction of High Street and Surrey Street

95. In 1926 the 'Broadway' commercial development took place at the corner of Surrey and High Street on the site of John Butts' orchard. The central feature was a small arcade leading to a cinema, between the present Pegrum's and Body Shop.

96. The north end of Surrey Street in 1990. Just this side of the large gabled building on the right (former Post Office) is the site of the *Norfolk Hotel*, demolished in 1959.

97. Vine Cottage, Church Street, dated 1727, is one of the surviving buildings from the old village of Littlehampton, and at a later date acquired a small Regency-style porch. Just visible (left) is the *Gratwicke Arms*, built in 1896, replacing the old *Spread Eagle Inn*.

98. Celebrations at the Manor House in March 1934, when the Urban District Council new headquarters opened there. The opening was performed by two local schoolchildren, Joan Strong and Eric Laker.

99. East Street looking towards Smarts Corner, in 1989. Set back (centre) is the *Spotted Cow*, a 1931 rebuild of the old *Cow Inn*. On the right the supermarket replaced the former Southdown garage (1927), closed in 1971.

100. Avon House, built
*c.*1800, near the *Gratwicke
Arms.* It was formerly a
priest's house, then an inn
(*Wheatsheaf*) and is now a
café. The cobble flint walls
have unfortunately been
painted.

101. The Flintstone Centre, East Street, was originally Littlehampton Elementary School, opened in 1878. The Centre is a good example of local flint and brick design, but has lost its Victorian main entrance tower and other details.

102.   Few towns can boast an 18th-century farm still working in an urban setting. 39 East Street is just that – an attractive flint and brick building dated 1772, with farmyard behind.

103.   The Old House, East Street. This is an 18th-century building in brick and flint, which was extensively remodelled between the wars. The construction of the ring road in 1976 did great harm to the setting of the house and the farm opposite.

104. Former Hampton House, East Street, once owned by Stephen Olliver, who died in 1883. By 1866 the house had become St Joseph's Apostolic College, and later St Joseph's Franciscan Convent and Home, which is still there today. Unhappily this historic building was completely rebuilt during 1968-71.

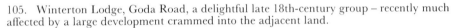

105. Winterton Lodge, Goda Road, a delightful late 18th-century group – recently much affected by a large development crammed into the adjacent land.

ROSEMEAD
LITTLEHAMPTON

□□

SCHOOL · FOR · GIRLS
(Recognised by the Board of Education)

Principals: RUTH A. YOUNG, B.A. Hons. Lond.

NITA E. E. SHARPE, Registered Teacher

Assisted by a fully-qualified Staff of resident and visiting teachers

The Matron is always a trained nurse.

106. Early advertisement (*c*.1930) for Rosemead School, showing the names of the founders, Miss Young and Miss Sharpe. The school has grown steadily in numbers and success since opening in 1919.

107. The Barn Arts Centre, East Street, is a fine late 18th-century barn, restored in 1978 by Rosemead School. It is now a venue for music and drama for both school and town use.

108. Pupils inspecting a bomb crater uncomfortably close to Rosemead School, during the Second World War.

109. Troops parading along Beach Road as part of 'War Weapons Week' in 1941.

110.   A volunteer fire brigade was established in Littlehampton in 1874. The picture shows the brigade outside the fire station in Maltravers Road in about 1930.

111. The V.E. Day street party held in Sandfield Avenue in 1945. Littlehampton was subjected to numerous air raids during the war. Twenty people were killed and 120 houses were destroyed or severely damaged.

112. The well-sited public library, Maltravers Road, was funded by Carnegie and designed by the Council's surveyor, H. Howard in a 'domestic Tudor style'. The foundation stone was laid by Lord Edmund Talbot, M.P.

This Foundation Stone
was laid by
Lord Edmund Talbot, M.P.
on the 4th March 1905.

113.   The well-sited war memorial was unveiled by General Lord Horne of Stirkoke in September 1921. To the right stands the monolithic Arun District Council Civic Centre, designed by W. H. Saunders & Son, and opened in 1986.

114.   The Rt. Hon. Nicholas Ridley M.P., then Minister of the Environment, opening the Arun District Council Civic Centre on 24 October 1986. The Centre, costing some £2.7 million, gave rise to controversy, many considering the building an inexcusable extravagance.

115. The new Roman Catholic church of St Catherine confronting St Mary's across open fields in about 1870. St Catherine's, designed by M. E. Hadfield in 1863, and enlarged in 1883 and 1904, was erected on land given by the Duke of Norfolk. The cost, nearly £4,000, was borne by the Duchess.

116. A number of attractive flint houses, with steeply pitched roofs and decorative barge boards, still survive in Littlehampton, forming a distinctive 'local style' and deserving preservation. Shown here are semi-detached examples in St Catherine's Road.

117. The Flint House,
Irvine Road – a fine example
of local building in flint,
dating from around 1880.

118. More houses in New Road in the handsome local flint vernacular – a photograph taken in about 1900. The house on the left is now a florist's shop.

119. In 1887 Maurice and Frederick Ockenden joined R. F. Duke, and in 1899 the above building in Terminus Road opened, bearing the logo 'Dando', i.e. D. and O. They are now widely-known water engineers.

120. Ockenden's was founded by William Ockenden in 1802 on a site near the north end of the Arcade. This portrait shows S. Howard Ockenden as Chairman of the Urban District Council in 1952.

121. A Duke and Ockenden advertisement of 1907, showing their 'Dando' air-lift pumping plant at Ford railway station.

122. The church of St James was built on the site of a mission chapel in 1908-9, in Arundel Road. It was designed by Frederick Wheeler and C. R. B. Godman, and became a parish church in 1929. This photograph shows the choir in about 1950. On the right is Frederick Walden-Aspy, M.A., vicar 1941-64. A devoted and much-loved priest, his great achievement was the building of a new church hall, opened in 1960. Father Aspy died in 1990, aged 86.

123. The sad end of Auklands, Norfolk Road, Convent School of the Holy Family, in 1988. The house was built by Charles Poland in 1885 and purchased by the Convent in 1914. It was the town's most successful independent school for many years.

124. Selborne Place, built by Robert Bushby in 1869, allegedly for descendants of Gilbert White. The houses form an attractive group with fashionable Gothic detailing, but have since suffered much from alteration, addition and neglect.

125. The Waterworks, St Flora's Road, with 91-ft. tower, was erected in 1880-2 by Grantham and Son. It remained in use until 1952 and was removed in 1961. The cottage (right) survives and the Parkside Evangelical Church (1973) now occupies the site.

126. The New Theatre in High Street, possibly the building opened by Trotter in 1807, the same year as his Theatre Royal, Worthing. Sited opposite the Congregational church, it was demolished in about 1897.

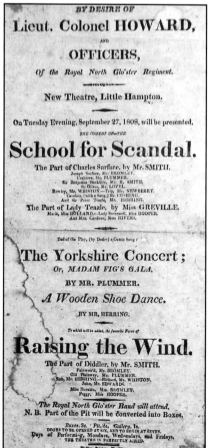

127. An early play-bill for the New Theatre. The North Gloucesters were manning the Battery at this time.

128.   A later play-bill dated 3 June 1825. The last recorded performance at the New Theatre was in 1852.

129.   In the 1890s Harry Joseph opened the Kursaal Theatre near the Arun Mill, the site later developed by Butlin's in 1931. The main attraction was Joseph's famous Pierrots, but by the late 1920s the theatre had become an amusement arcade.

130. Harry Joseph's Arcadia Company. These players were the mainstay of Littlehampton's entertainment for many years and were immensely popular with locals and visitors alike.

Harry Joseph's Pierrots

WINNERS OF THE
Great Palladium Concert Party Contest

Early in July, 1911, the "London Evening Times" started a competition among Pierrot and other Concert Parties of four or more performers. More than sixty parties were in the competition. The ten securing the largest number of votes were invited to attend a matinee at the London Palladium on September 28th, 1911.

HARRY JOSEPH'S PARTY RECEIVED
——— NEARLY 20,000 VOTES ———

At the Palladium before a great committee of Theatre and Music Hall Magnates, and a **Record Audience of more than 5000 Persons**

HARRY JOSEPH'S PIERROT PARTY
WERE DECLARED THE WINNERS

They immediately received an engagement for the London Palladium, and during the following week were booked for a number of other halls.

"An Entertainment that everyone enjoys"—*Vide Press*

131. Harry Joseph's promotional advertisement announcing his company's success in the 'Grand Palladium Concert Party Contest' of 1911.

132. The former St Saviour's church, New Road, erected in 1877. Ten years later it served as a theatre (Jubilee Hall) and was often used by Harry Joseph, but in 1898 was occupied by the Methodists. The building was demolished in 1980.

133. Harry Joseph's popular Pierrot Concert Party. For a time Joseph leased Jubilee Hall (St Saviour's) in New Road (now Church House flats) and it became the venue for numerous entertainments.

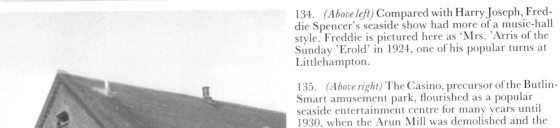

134. *(Above left)* Compared with Harry Joseph, Freddie Spencer's seaside show had more of a music-hall style. Freddie is pictured here as 'Mrs. 'Arris of the Sunday 'Erold' in 1924, one of his popular turns at Littlehampton.

135. *(Above right)* The Casino, precursor of the Butlin-Smart amusement park, flourished as a popular seaside entertainment centre for many years until 1930, when the Arun Mill was demolished and the whole site developed by Butlin's.

136. *(Left)* The Palladium cinema, Church Street, some two years before demolition in 1986. Built by Linfield and Sons, the hall opened in 1910 as the Olympic Skating Rink, becoming the Empire Theatre and cinema in around 1912, and Palladium in 1920.

BUTLIN'S
Windmill Amusement Park
LITTLEHAMPTON,
SUSSEX-BY-THE-SEA.

HERE YOU HAVE THE FINEST AMUSEMENT PARK ON THE SOUTH COAST.

THE THRILLER (Figure Eight) takes you on "Top of the World."
The DODGEM ELECTRIC CARS. WATER SPEED BOATS.
THE CATERPILLAR. THE NOAH'S ARK. HONEYMOON
EXPRESS. MIRROR MAZE. THE WOBBLEMS.
KIDDIES' RIDES, etc., etc.

REALLY A WONDERFUL VARIETY OF PLEASURE.

THERE IS PLENTY OF SHELTER FOR EVERYONE.

WHEN IT'S WET OR FINE — VISIT BUTLIN'S.

Special Prices for Conducted Parties and Outings ——— Write Manager.

137. An early advertisement for Butlin's 'Windmill Amusement Park', opened in 1931 after the sale of the mill site in 1930. Without a doubt the Park brought prosperity to Littlehampton, but environmentally the cost was high – unsightly buildings dominating a very sensitive and scenic area of the town.

138. The former Odeon in High Street, designed by the leading cinema architect Andrew Mather in 1931. It was built on the site of The Lodge, once occupied by Thomas Constable. The Odeon, latterly a bingo hall, was demolished in 1984.

139. Outdoor entertainment by the popular 'Pierrot Folk' troupe on a temporary stage set up near the Coastguard Station in the early 1930s.

140. The Windmill Theatre. Built as a 'Shelter Hall' in 1912, it became exclusively a theatre organised by the L.U.D.C. entertainments manager, Charles Dore, *c*.1927. In 1968 it was refurbished as the 'Western Pavilion', and in 1973 again renamed – 'Windmill Theatre' – incorporating a cinema and restaurant.

141. Some of Smart's latest amusements have been erected on the site of the old Battery, which was constructed in 1759-60 to protect the harbour. The armament consisted of seven 18-pound guns, later dismantled *c*.1833. The land was sold for coastguard use.

142. Once a prominent feature on the Green – the bandstand at the end of Banjo Road. To the south stood the large pavilion where there was dancing to Phil Simmons' band, and on wet days the Pierrot Folk entertained. The buildings were demolished in 1968.

143. Littlehampton cricket team, founded in 1871, photographed during a match at Arundel in 1889, when the result was a tie.

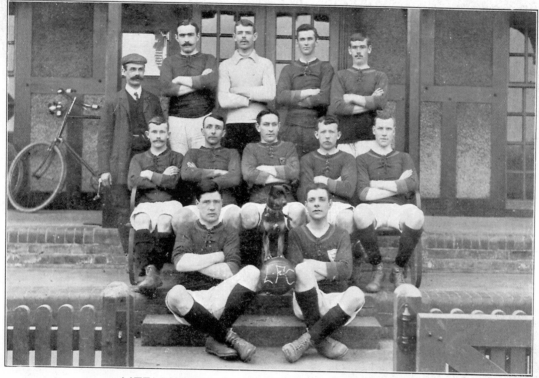

LITTLEHAMPTON FOOTBALL TEAM, 1906-7.

Reading from left to right the names are:—First Row—F. Rose, E. Sewell, D. Carpenter, R. Linfield, S. Tate; Second Row—G. Creese, G. Batchelor, A. Holland, G. Price, H. Swift; Third Row—Waterhouse, H. Woolven.

Photo by Spry, Littlehampton.

144.   A promotional giant postcard depicting the Littlehampton Football Team of 1906-7.

145.   Littlehampton Golf Club marooned by floods in 1913. The Club was formed in 1889 and a building erected in 1894, which was burned down in 1985. A new Clubhouse designed by James Bell, a former Club Captain, was opened by the Duchess of Norfolk in 1987.

146.   The famous Pashley brothers with other flying enthusiasts at the Littlehampton Aviation Meeting held in August 1913. The brothers had founded their Aero Club at Shoreham the previous year; the aircraft is a Henri Farman biplane.

147.   Littlehampton's first railway station opened in 1863 on a branch from the Brighton to Portsmouth line. The building followed a standard pattern – similar to Hove, Arundel and West Worthing. It was demolished on electrification in 1938, and not permanently replaced for 49 years.

148.   J. V. Rastrick's railway 'drawbridge' constructed over the Arun at Ford in 1846, the contractor being 'Mr. Butt of Littlehampton'. Reconstructed in steel in 1862, the bridge was fixed in position in 1938.

149.   The locomotive 'Littlehampton', No. 172, was a Class B. I. Billinton-modified 'Gladstone', built at Brighton in 1891, and withdrawn in 1933. In November 1922 she was involved in a derailment at Windmill Bridge Junction.

150.   Southern Railway's 0-6-0 tank 2233 being serviced outside the Littlehampton engine shed in about 1930. The shed, now restored and listed, is the only part of the original 1863 station now surviving. Behind is the old police station, now the site of Madehurst Court.

151. Littlehampton station's signal box dates from the 1860s and is now one of the few original examples surviving after British Rail's wholesale destruction of similar buildings in 1988.

152. The new railway station was opened in 1987; it replaced a 'temporary' timber structure, a notorious eyesore – erected in 1938.

153. The much-altered Thorncroft Cottage, Horsham Road, dates from before 1700, and at one time was used as a café.

154. Rural Wick in 1901. Housing development began in the area following the construction of the railway in 1863. The main builder was J. C. Pepper, and the new Beconsfield Road and North Street Area was dubbed 'Pepperville'.

155. An early view of All Saints' Mission Church, Wick, designed by a leading Victorian architect G. E. Street in 1881. The chimney has now gone and the west doorway blocked.

156. The Old Cottage, Wick Street, is a fine, traditional flint building dated 1736. On the extreme right the original *True Blue Inn* can just be seen, later rebuilt in the 1930s.

157. Duke and Ockenden's workforce laying the water main in Wick Street in 1898. On the left is Vine Cottage (1888) which still stands today, just north of the modern Wick shopping parade.

158.   Procession of Wick schoolchildren en route to the opening of the new swing bridge on 27 May 1908.

159.   Recent industrial development
on the northern fringe of Wick,
showing the disruptive effect of such
building in a residential environment.

160.   Lyminster crossing *c*.1900 is the site of the former Arundel and Littlehampton Station, which was briefly the terminus of the L.B.S.C.R. line to Portsmouth, in 1846. The station closed in 1863 but during 1907-14 Lyminster Halt was in use. Remains of the old station were demolished *c*.1978.

161.   The former *Windmill and Signal Inn* and Slator's grocer's shop at Lyminster crossing in about 1905. Both buildings remain today but with changed uses.

162. The *Locomotive Inn* at Lyminster crossing was built *c.*1850 by John Eede Butt to serve the railway station which existed nearby along Coomes Way (1846-63). The inn is a listed building and its attractive cobble flint exterior has so far not been disfigured by paint.

163. The Old Coach House was at one time the stables to Court Wick Park. It was built *c.*1820 in a delightful Gothic style, with clocktower and pineapple finials on the gate piers.

164. Forge Cottage, Lyminster Road, a picturesque thatched cottage of *c.*1720, which remained a blacksmith's until around 1932.

165. The flint and brick *Six Bells Inn* stands on the Lyminster Road close to Forge Cottage and the Black Ditch, and is dated 1732.

166. The ancient Toddington Farmhouse, Toddington Lane. The south end is 16th-century, the north 19th-century, both with stepped gables – unusual in Sussex. The adjacent dovecote is dated 1699.

167. Toddington House, Toddington Lane, perhaps the finest listed building in the Littlehampton area, dates from about 1600. It is timber framed, and clad with flint and brick with an elegant octagonal stone chimney. The house was restored by George Upjohn in 1958.

168. St Mary's, Clymping, an excellent example of 13th-century church architecture built by John de Clymping, Bishop of Chichester in 1253. The church contains a series of paintings, 'Christ's Coming', by Heyward Hardy (1932). Ford Prison, just to the north, has much harmed the setting of the church.

169. Clymping Vicarage, now Church House, is an attractive example of stucco Gothic style by W. F. Pocock, c.1833.

170. Clymping smock mill replaced an earlier one in 1799, and worked until c.1900. Later, owned by Sir Richard Garton, it was converted into a dwelling with dummy sweeps in the 1920s. In 1962 the upper sections were removed and a distinctive landmark lost.

171. Clymping School, near Brookpits, was one of Robert Busby's later commissions, dated 1878. This pleasant example of a small village school has so far survived threats of closure and some 80 children attend at present.

172.   Brookpits, just off the A259 at Clymping, a fine example of a yeoman's house *c*.1650. Built in local flint with brick dressing the house has a two-storeyed porch and mullioned windows.

173. Bailiffscourt was originally the residence of the bailiff of Séez Abbey in Normandy and the small chapel shown here (*c*.1270) alone survives on the original site. The surrounding buildings, some imported from elsewhere, date from 1935 and were erected by Lord Moyne and his architect, Amyas Phillips.

174. The late 13th-century chapel at Bailiffscourt showing an interior view of the three-light east window, enriched with fine foliage carving on the capitals.

175. Mewsbrook, later the *Rustington Towers Hotel*, stood until 1935 near the present boating lake. It was an essay in a Gothic style by the local architect Robert Busby for a Mr. Barnes in about 1865.

176.   The elegant Wren-style Rustington Convalescent Home, just east of Mewsbrook, was designed by Frederick Wheeler in 1897. Its founder Sir Henry Harben (1823-1911), High Sheriff of Sussex, was Master of the Worshipful Company of Carpenters, who now run the Home.

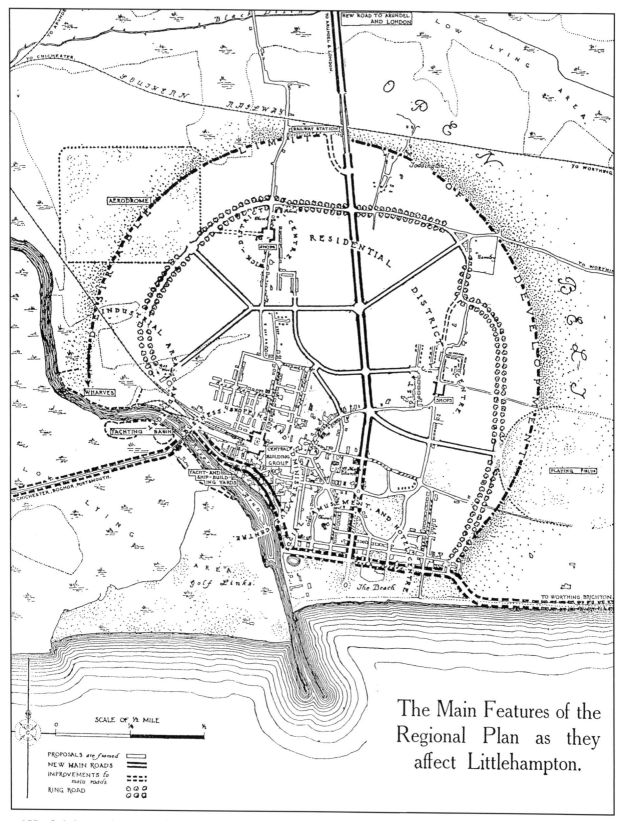

The Main Features of the Regional Plan as they affect Littlehampton.

SCALE OF ½ MILE

PROPOSALS are framed
NEW MAIN ROADS
IMPROVEMENTS to main roads
RING ROAD

177. It is interesting to consider this 'Regional Plan' of 1929 in view of the recently projected developments in Littlehampton. Note the proposals for the West Bank, the 'Limit of Development', the Aerodrome and especially the preservation of a 'Green Belt' east of the town.

Some Dates in Littlehampton's History

1139	Queen Matilda landed from France in an attempt to seize the English throne from her son King Stephen.
	*c.*1574 Henry Fitzalan, Earl of Arundel, said to have embanked lower section of the Arun.
1586	Philip, Earl of Arundel, arrested at Littlehampton en route to the Low Countries, to raise an army to invade England.
1633	William Cotham's Survey of Toddington Lands (including Littlehampton Manor).
1732	Act for Erecting Piers (Littlehampton Harbour Act).
1759	Battery established on east bank.
1790	Fifth Earl of Berkeley built a house a little east of the present Norfolk Place, to become Surrey House in 1820.
1793	Towpath to Arundel authorised.
1802	Ockendens founded.
	Bath House erected near Beach Hotel.
1807	The New Theatre in High Street opened by Thomas Trotter.
1820	Earl of Berkeley's house (Surrey House purchased by Earl of Surrey.
1824	Ferry Act passed. Opened 1825.
1831	Arun Mill near Oyster Pond built by Henry Martin.
1834	Petition for transfer of Custom House from Arundel to Littlehampton refused.
1841	Survey of Littlehampton harbour published by Henry Salter.
1843	Littlehampton Port Survey presented to Parliament by W. B. Prichard.
1846	Timber railway bridge erected at Ford.
1847	First gas-works built in Pier Road.
1853	Local Board of Health established. The Rev. John Atkyns was first chairman.
1854	Fort built on west bank.
1863	Railway station opened.
	Cross-Channel steamboat service begun.
1867-8	Construction of the Esplanade.
1868	Roman Catholic School opened. Site now St Catherine's Court; school removed to Highdown Drive (1973).
1869	Town's first newspaper, *The News*, published; later called *Littlehampton News*; closed in 1914.
1871	Littlehampton Cricket Club formed.
1877	Harvey's barque *Trossachs* launched.
1882	Henry Lock (1806-95) gave a lecture on Littlehampton's history.
1884	Lifeboat station opened. First boat, *Undaunted*, ex-Chichester Harbour.
1887	Loop line opened at Ford Junction to connect with mid-Sussex line.
1893	Littlehampton Urban District created.
1895	Connaught Road School opened.
	Death of Henry Lock.
1897	Rustington Convalescent Home opened.
	Nelson Inn rebuilt, completing the west end of seafront.

1901	Wick, formerly part of Lyminster parish, added to Littlehampton.
1904	Lifeboat *Brothers Freeman* launched by Duchess of Norfolk.
	Extension of esplanade completed.
1905	Referendum on building a swing bridge.
1906	Public library opened on land given by the Duke of Norfolk.
1907	Seventy-eight fishing boats registered at Littlehampton, employing 154 men and boys.
1908	New Swing Bridge opened.
1910	Olympic Skating Rink (later cinema) opened.
1911	Littlehampton Hospital opened.
1914	Convent of the Holy Family opened a school at Auklands, Norfolk Road.
1919	Rosemead School founded by Miss R. A. Young and Miss Nita Sharpe.
1922	Arcade and related buildings erected on site of the old Eagle Stores.
1926	Museum opened as annexe to public library, mainly funded by a bequest from Alan Thompson of Littlehampton.
1927	Littlehampton Harbour and River Arun Drainage Outfall Act authorised Harbour Board to spend £72,000 on improvements.
1931	Duke of Norfolk sold much of Littlehampton to Percy Harvey Estates.
	Population reaches 10,435.
	Butlin's Amusement Park opened.
1933	Last Fair Day in Surrey Street.
1934	Manor House became Council Offices.
	Commemorative plaque designed by Mrs. W. H. Clarkson erected to mark position of town pump (Manor House car park entrance).
1936	The Plantation renamed Lobs Wood.
1937	Electrification of railway to Littlehampton.
1938	Mewsbrook boating lake opened.
1940	18 August: Ford aerodrome bombed.
1944	September – promenade re-opened.
1948	Surrey House demolished.
1951	Romano-British settlement discovered at Wickbourne Estate.
1956	Glasshouse Crops Research Institute opened by the Duke of Norfolk.
1959	*Norfolk Hotel*, Surrey Street, demolished.
	Ford Royal Navy Air Station (HMS *Peregrine*) closed.
1962	Death of Charles Butt, last survivor of the Butt family.
	New Arun Yacht Club building opened.
1964	Van Heyningen's nursery established at Toddington.
1966	New museum opened in River Road by Claude Muncaster.
1967	New police station opened.
1971	The Old Granary (1731), East Street, restored and re-erected at the Weald and Downland Museum.
1972	Amalgamation of Andrew Cairns and Maude Allan schools.
1973	New road bridge over the Arun opened.
	Wick shopping centre opened.
1974	Littlehampton gains a Town Council. Geoffrey J. Hollis is first mayor.
1977	Smart's take over Butlin's.
1979	New lifeboat house opened.

1981	Population 17,228.
	High Street pedestrianised.
1982	'Twinning' ceremonies took place in Littlehampton (30 October) and Chennevières-sur-Marne (2 October).
	New footbridge over the Arun opened.
1983	Robinson family exhibition held at Littlehampton Museum.
1985	Death of Jack Thompson; local historian.
1986	New Arun District Council offices opened.
1987	New railway station opened.
1988	Twinning ceremony (23 April) with Durmersheim (Germany).
1989	Arun District Council's *Local Draft Plan* published.
1990	Removal of Institute of Horticultural Research to Warwickshire announced.
	Permission to demolish Floyd's Corner refused at public enquiry.
1991	Museum moved to the Manor House.